Date: 5/18/18

BR 595.752 PER
Perish, Patrick,
Aphids /

INSECTS
UP CLOSE

Aphids

by Patrick Perish

Note to Librarians, Teachers, and Parents:

Blastoff! Readers are carefully developed by literacy experts and combine standards-based content with developmentally appropriate text.

Level 1 provides the most support through repetition of high-frequency words, light text, predictable sentence patterns, and strong visual support.

Level 2 offers early readers a bit more challenge through varied simple sentences, increased text load, and less repetition of high-frequency words.

Level 3 advances early-fluent readers toward fluency through increased text and concept load, less reliance on visuals, longer sentences, and more literary language.

Level 4 builds reading stamina by providing more text per page, increased use of punctuation, greater variation in sentence patterns, and increasingly challenging vocabulary.

Level 5 encourages children to move from "learning to read" to "reading to learn" by providing even more text, varied writing styles, and less familiar topics.

Whichever book is right for your reader, Blastoff! Readers are the perfect books to build confidence and encourage a love of reading that will last a lifetime!

This edition first published in 2018 by Bellwether Media, Inc.

No part of this publication may be reproduced in whole or in part without written permission of the publisher. For information regarding permission, write to Bellwether Media, Inc., Attention: Permissions Department, 5357 Penn Avenue South, Minneapolis, MN 55419.

Library of Congress Cataloging-in-Publication Data

Names: Perish, Patrick.
Title: Aphids / by Patrick Perish.
Description: Minneapolis, MN : Bellwether Media, Inc., 2018. | Series:
    Blastoff! Readers. Insects Up Close | Audience: Age 5-8. | Audience: K to
    grade 3. | Includes bibliographical references and index.
Identifiers: LCCN 2016052743 (print) | LCCN 2016053546 (ebook) | ISBN
    9781626176584 (hardcover : alk. paper) | ISBN 9781681033884 (ebook)
Subjects: LCSH: Aphids–Juvenile literature.
Classification: LCC QL527.A64 P46 2018 (print) | LCC QL527.A64 (ebook) | DDC
    595.7/52–dc23
LC record available at https://lccn.loc.gov/2016052743

Editor: Christina Leighton   Designer: Maggie Rosier

Printed in the United States of America, North Mankato, MN.

Table of Contents

What Are Aphids?

Aphids are tiny pests. These insects suck plant **sap**.

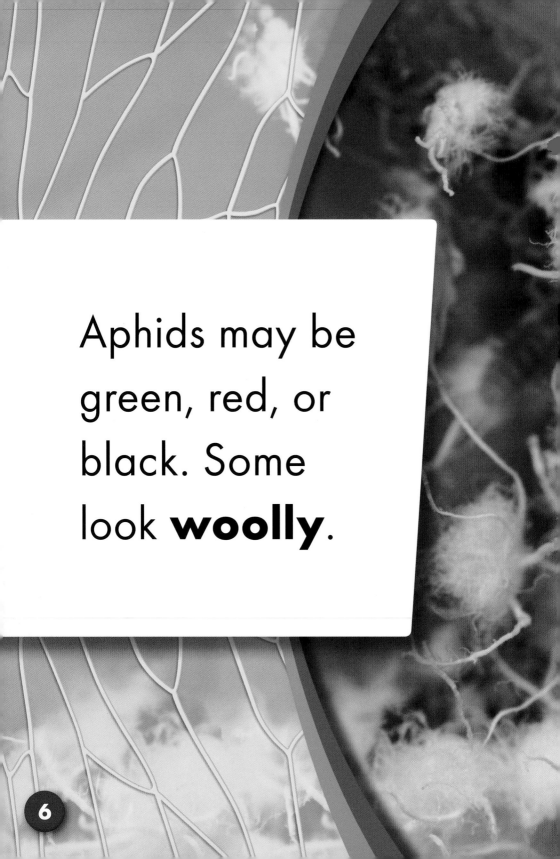

Aphids may be green, red, or black. Some look **woolly**.

woolly aphids

ACTUAL
SIZE:
giant bark aphid

Aphids have short **tubes** on their backs. Drops come out of them to warn others of danger.

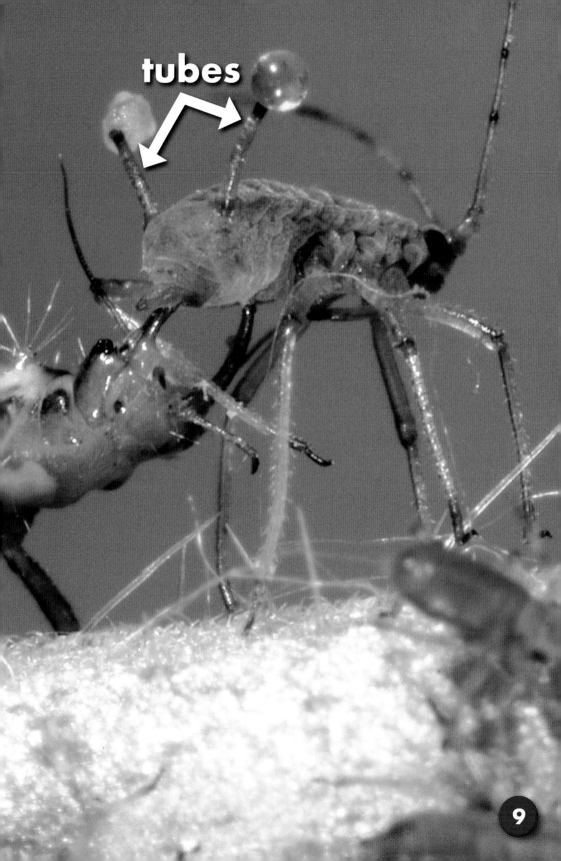

tubes

Plants, Poop, and Pests

Aphids live on trees and **crops**. One plant can hold many aphids.

FAVORITE
FOOD:

plant sap

Aphids poop **honeydew**. Ants collect it and eat it!

ant

honeydew

13

Ladybugs and earwigs eat aphids. They help control the pests.

ladybug

Growing Up

Aphids both give birth and lay eggs. They give birth in warm weather.

APHID LIFE SPAN:
about 1 month

aphid giving
birth

Aphids lay eggs
when it gets cold.
The babies break
out in spring.

eggs

Young aphids can make plants too crowded. Aphids with wings fly to new plants. Time to eat!

wings

Glossary

crops

plants grown by farmers

tubes

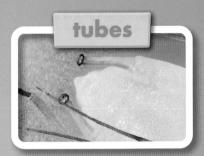

long, rounded body parts

honeydew

the sweet liquid some insects make from feeding on plants

woolly

to look like wool, a soft and hairy material

sap

watery juices from a plant

To Learn More

AT THE LIBRARY

Mattern, Joanne. *It's a Good Thing There Are Ladybugs*. New York, N.Y.: Children's Press, 2015.

Perish, Patrick. *Earwigs*. Minneapolis, Minn.: Bellwether Media, 2018.

Rustad, Martha E. H. *Ants and Aphids Work Together*. Mankato, Minn.: Capstone Press, 2011.

ON THE WEB

Learning more about aphids is as easy as 1, 2, 3.

1. Go to www.factsurfer.com.

2. Enter "aphids" into the search box.

3. Click the "Surf" button and you will see a list of related web sites.

With factsurfer.com, finding more information is just a click away.

Index